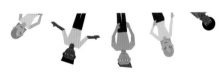

HONOR HEAD

Franklin Watts
Published in paperback in Great Britain in 2019 by The Watts Publishing Group

Credits:
Consultant: Ratna Dutt, OBE, Chief Executive, Race Equality Foundation
Series Editor: Jean Coppendale
Series Designer: Lorraine Inglis


Picture credits:
Every attempt has been made to clear copyright. Should there be any inadvertent omission please apply to the publisher for rectification.
t = top,  b = bottom ,  l = left,  r = right,  m = middle
All images listed here are © Shutterstock: cover and 12–13 Creatarka/4 Decorwithme/5 and talking heads throughout DreamMaster/6–7 background Magenta10; 6b KannaA/7t snapgalleria;  bluebird file404; Muhammad Ali Featureflash Photo Agency/8 OnBlast/ 9bl Tetiana Yurchenko/10 Evellean/13 Tinie Tempah Featureflash Photo Agency/14 dednniro/15t Studio G/16–17 background Mikhail Klyoshev/18 folder Axstokes; red seal billdayone/19bl Yu Zhdanova/20 background Oleynik Aline/22–23 world Jemstock/ 23 Taylor Swift Tinseltown/24 background dreams3d/25t Dacian G/26t jesadaphorn; b Emeraldora/27br Candy Duck/28 background kampolz; birds Mrs. Opossum


ISBN 978 1 4451 5287 5


Printed in China

Franklin Watts
an imprint of
Hachette Children's Group
part of The Watts Publishing Group
Carmelite House
50 Victoria Embankment
London EC4Y 0DZ

An Hachette UK Company
www.hachette.co.uk

www.franklinwatts.co.uk

# Contents

Guten tag!

# WHAT IS CULTURE?

The word culture has many meanings and can include everything from the food we eat and the clothes we wear, to our religious beliefs and everyday values.

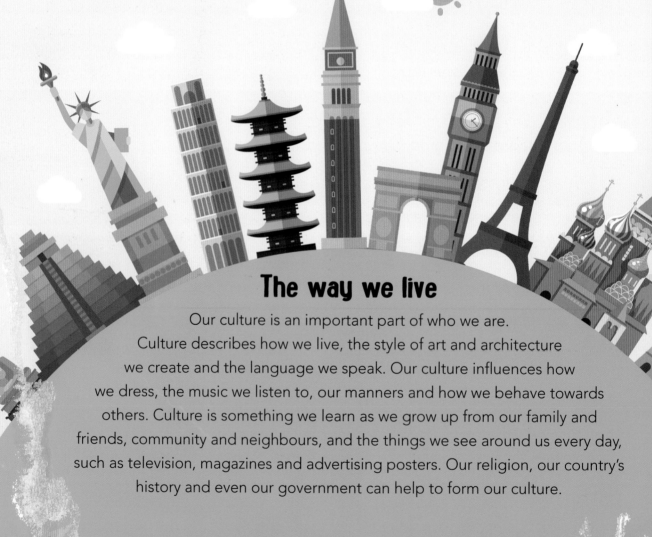

## The way we live

Our culture is an important part of who we are. Culture describes how we live, the style of art and architecture we create and the language we speak. Our culture influences how we dress, the music we listen to, our manners and how we behave towards others. Culture is something we learn as we grow up from our family and friends, community and neighbours, and the things we see around us every day, such as television, magazines and advertising posters. Our religion, our country's history and even our government can help to form our culture.

# The same but different

There can be many different groups or denominations within the same religion. They may worship in a different way or have different rules or ways of behaviour. For example, Orthodox Jews strictly follow the ancient laws of Judaism, while Reform Jews see the ancient laws as more of a guide for how to live in today's world.

Both have the same beliefs but their culture and way of behaving is different.

For some denominations, the difference is based on their interpretation of their holy book. Muslim Sunnis and Shi'as both believe in the teachings of the Qur'an, but each has a different interpretation of part of the teachings.

## Religious wars

There have been religious wars throughout history. Followers of nearly every religion have gone to war to fight for their beliefs and to protect their followers and way of life when it has been threatened by oppression or discrimination. But some religious followers will fight to impose their beliefs on others because they believe that is what their holy book tells them to do, or because it may be a way of gaining power.

*Rivers, ponds, lakes and streams – they all have different names, but they all contain water. Just as religions do – they all contain truths.*

Muhammad Ali (1942–2016), champion boxer

# CULTURE AND LAW

Every country has laws. The laws are there to protect the rights of the citizens and to uphold the beliefs of the country.

## Changing laws

The laws of a country protect the people who live there. For many countries, the laws are in place to allow people their freedom and human rights – laws such as it is wrong to kill, to deliberately injure or hurt another person, to keep anyone imprisoned and to steal. But countries and their people are constantly changing and developing as a result of social issues, scientific discoveries, humanitarian issues and immigration. For example, laws relating to hate crimes, such as racism and homophobia, have become tighter in recent years to reflect our changing attitudes, and many countries have introduced new laws or adapted existing laws to take into account crimes such as cyberbullying and computer hacking.

## Law and religion

In some countries the law and religion are very closely connected, and one often influences the other. The laws in Muslim countries, from what to eat and wear to how to conduct financial dealings, are based on the teachings of the Prophet Muhammad (pbuh) as written in the Qur'an.

Most religions have their own rules and rituals that believers follow but these are not always laws that have been set down by the government. Most of us behave in a certain way because that is part of our culture – the way we've been brought up and taught to behave.

## A new country

When someone migrates they have to obey the laws of their new country. Accepting new laws can be difficult and confusing especially if they are very different from those of the country of origin. What is acceptable in the old country can be illegal in a new country and this may create a conflict with a person's original beliefs and traditions. But it is the responsibility of those moving to a new country to keep the laws of that country. These laws are there to give everyone equal levels of freedom and protection.

**TALKBACK!**

If immigrants in a new country have to accept laws that conflict with their religion or cultural beliefs, how do you think they might feel?

I think religious rules and laws are stronger than a country's laws.

In a new country you have to accept the law of that country, even if it means going against your religion.

# A CHANGING SOCIETY

Multiculturalism can be positive and energising for society but it can also lead to differences between generations and to people feeling isolated.

## Them and us

It can be difficult for first-generation migrants to adapt and change. It is often easier for generations born and brought up in the adopted country to blend their own cultural beliefs with the values of the indigenous culture. But some young people from black and minority ethnic families fear the loss of their original cultural identity and this can create conflict. They may reject the country they now live in, especially if they feel their original beliefs are not respected, or they may have no sense of belonging and feel alienated by the culture of the adopted country.

## Changing culture

As we become more multicultural so our society changes. Sometimes we change laws, but mostly we change attitudes and the mainstream culture develops to include elements of other cultures, for example in fashion or music. But some minority ethnic communities may not feel part of the wider community for a variety of reasons, and remain feeling isolated, outside of the mainsteam culture.

# A multicultural society

A walk down the high street can often reveal the effect multiculturalism has on a local community with Polish, Asian, Caribbean and Indian food stores and restaurants and places of worship, such as synagogues, mosques and temples.

But true multiculturalism comes when different societies accept and tolerate each other's beliefs and values and everyone feels that they are an important and valued part of the country they live in.

**TALKBACK!**

Do you think that becoming a multicultural society can mean a country may lose its own identity or can it make it better?

*It seems we have to change our traditions so that we don't offend anyone else, which means we'll lose our own identity.*

*But all this new stuff is part of our true identity now. The old and the new can work side by side. I love Diwali as much as Guy Fawkes night.*

# STEREOTYPING

Stereotyping is when a person is judged on the way that person looks or dresses, how they speak or where he or she comes from.

## Stereotyping is wrong

Judging someone purely on the way they look, what they wear or where they come from is lazy and ignorant. Stereotyping is like saying that all men should be good at football and that all women should be good at baking. Not very realistic or accurate! Some stereotyping, such as racial stereotyping, is very harmful and can cause tension and lead to violence.

## Why does stereotyping happen?

Making general judgements about people is easy. It means we don't have to think about them as individuals – we can just see that they wear a turban, or a short dress, or have tattoos and give them a 'label'. Stereotypes are generally created by different cultures through prejudice. Blogs, online videos, newspapers and television can all reinforce stereotypes until we start to label people without even realising what we're doing. We might also use stereotypes to fit in with the beliefs of our peer group or family. It's very hard to stand alone if you don't agree when everyone around you is saying the same thing.

# Who stereotypes?

Stereotyping can happen in all cultures and the form it takes depends on the culture and beliefs. Strict Muslims might assume that a girl wearing a short dress is immoral because the Muslim dress code for women is very different. Some people might label all Muslims as anti-West because they only ever hear about Muslims as terrorists.

## Make up your own mind

- When you see something online, in a newspaper or on television, question where it comes from. Is the author reliable and informed or does the message sound unbalanced and prejudiced? Is the piece based on stereotypes or promoting a stereotype?

- Don't just agree when family or friends make a comment about a person based on what they look like. Ask them to explain why they are making that assumption – often people make a judgement without thinking about it.

*At the end of the day, I'm a human being and I just think that's what it is. Challenging stereotypes by just being who I am.*

Tinie Tempah (b. 1988), singer, songwriter and record producer

# Old v. new

Migrants often have a tough time settling into their new home. They feel that their values and beliefs are threatened and misunderstood. But later generations have their own issues and conflicts to face.

## All change

People choose to migrate for many different reasons. Some want a better lifestyle and job opportunities for themselves and their children but many are forced to leave their country as a result of war or religious or political persecution. These immigrants can be deeply sad at having to leave their home and country; some have been traumatised by war and are confused and frightened at suddenly being in a new country that is so different from their own. They may struggle to integrate and only feel safe with people from the same background.

## A new generation

It can be hard to adapt to new ways, especially for older people. Their values, traditions and culture are part of who they are and they stick to what they know and believe. Second- and even third-generation migrants can often feel caught in the middle of the culture of their parents and grandparents and that of their adopted country. Culture clashes can happen when the older generations struggle to maintain their original customs and values and the younger generations strive to adapt to the ways of their friends and peers.

> **Being caught between two cultures can be confusing.**
> **What do you think of these points of view?**

My parents don't understand what it is like to feel different at school. They've never experienced that.

I fit in with the family at home – I really like some of our traditions. When I'm with friends, I switch to my new culture.

My parents are upset by the way I behave sometimes, but that's the way it is here. They have to accept that.

My grandparents love their old culture but this is the only culture I've ever known.

# Integrating

Many first-generation migrants have grown up speaking their original language at home and behaving in a way that follows their family values, and then speaking English in school and learning different values. These young people can feel torn and resentful towards their family for 'holding them back' or not allowing them to fully integrate with their new culture. Some might feel that they are neither one culture nor the other. If you feel this way, talk to a trusted adult about it, maybe a family member, a teacher, or someone from your religious community, or contact a helpline (see page 31).

## Defending your beliefs

In a democratic society everyone has the right to follow the religion of their choice and to defend their beliefs. No one should be bullied or pressurised into adopting the religion of their new country or to abandon religion altogether. However, it is against the law to endanger or injure anyone in the name of religion, or to help anyone else to do this.

# CLASHES at home

Being a teenager is a challenging time for most young people. For teens caught between two cultures, it can be especially hard. Here are some ways to cope with cultural differences within your family.

## Talk to your parents

It can seem very unfair when your parents, older brothers, uncles or grandparents criticise you or your friends, or you feel that you don't have the same freedom as your peers. But most families only want what they believe is the best for you. They want to protect you and keep you safe. Set aside a time to sit down with your family and talk to them about how you feel. And listen to what is worrying them. Reassure them that you don't behave in the way they see some other young people behaving that upsets and alarms them.

## Still a believer

Many rules about dress and behaviour stem from religious values. If you are breaking these rules your family might be fearful that you are turning your back on your religion. Explain that you can still keep your faith without having to follow all the old rules. Reassure them that there are many things about your old culture and religion that you love and respect and that you feel you can combine the two cultures.

# Be understanding

Don't accuse your family of being old-fashioned or worse! Don't attack their culture or beliefs … they have every right to believe what they choose to, just as you do. Respect their choices. Explain that you are not being deliberately disrespectful to their beliefs or culture, but help them to understand that as you've grown up in a different country and culture your feelings about things are different.

# A better life

Your parents or grandparents probably decided to migrate so they could give their children a better life, not to leave their culture behind. Leaving their homeland was probably one of the biggest and hardest decisions they have ever made and they may have made it for the benefit of their family.

## 'The Talk' check list

☑ Stay calm, don't shout or walk out in a temper. If people become angry, continue the discussion another time.

☑ This is a talk to understand each other, not an excuse to criticise everything you hate in your life. Treat your parents' viewpoints with respect.

☑ Listen to how the adults see things – maybe they have misunderstood what they've seen or heard about young people always getting into trouble.

☑ It is unlikely the adults will change their mind about their expectations of you. See if you can come to a compromise that suits you both.

# YOUR RIGHTS MATTER

Everyone has the right to feel safe at home, in their community and where they go to school. But some families have cultural beliefs that can threaten a child's safety.

## Not so safe at home

Sadly, children of all backgrounds can experience hurt and abuse at home, at school and in their community by people who know that what they are doing is wrong. But in some homes children are hurt by certain practices that their family consider to be part of their traditional way of life. Female circumcision, also called female genital mutilation (FGM), is part of many cultures worldwide. It is carried out on girls from infancy to about 15 years of age or just before puberty in the belief that it will increase a girl's chance of a good marriage. FGM has no health advantages at all, is extremely painful and results in permanent injury that will be a problem for the girl for the rest of her life. It can also cause death through infection and other complications.

FGM is illegal in the UK and USA and it is illegal to take a child out of the UK for FGM to be done in another country. If you know someone who is being threatened with FGM, or who has had it done and needs proper medical care, there are many organisations that can help (see page 31). It is nothing to be ashamed of and no one is going to be disgusted or judge you. Speak to your teacher, doctor, school nurse, the police or helpline. Your information will be treated with respect.

# A forced marriage

We all have the right to choose if we want to get married, who we want to marry, and when and where. A forced marriage in law is defined as being when you face physical violence or psychological or emotional pressure, such as bringing shame or dishonour to the family, if you don't go through with a marriage. Boys as well as girls can be forced to marry.

Some young people are tricked into going abroad to visit family and then forced to marry against their will, but forced marriages often take place at home as well. Young people forced into a marriage feel that they have lost control of their lives – they feel helpless and as if their life is over.

*Forced marriage* is not the same as an **arranged marriage**, which is done with the **full consent** of everyone involved.

## Not alone

If you have been or are being threatened with a forced marriage there are lots of places to go for help. Go to your local police station or speak to a trusted adult. There are lots of helplines, too (see page 31). ChildLine reports that their calls rose by 30 per cent in 2015 and more than half their callers were 15 or under and some as young as nine. Your call will be treated in full confidence.

## TIP

The charity Karma Nirvana (see page 31) advises girls forced to go abroad to marry to hide a metal spoon in their underwear. This will set off the alarm as they go through customs and give them a chance to tell someone official what is happening to them.

# I am what I wear

The clothes we choose to wear are often a statement about who we are. For some cultures, clothes also say a lot about their beliefs and values.

## School uniform

We have school uniforms to create a feeling of belonging to the school, to ensure appropriate clothing is being worn for exercise classes and school trips and to stop children being bullied or feeling embarrassed if they can't afford fashionable clothing.

Most schools have strict rules about school uniform that everyone, no matter what their religion or culture, should follow. However, some religions also have dress codes that reflect their beliefs and values, such as wearing a patak, headscarf or crucifix. Because it is a cultural not a legal requirement, the school can refuse permission for these to be worn if it is against school rules.

## Find a compromise

There may be many reasons why a school refuses permission for a student to wear a certain item of clothing, and legal guidelines advise the school to balance the rights of individual pupils against the interests of the school as a whole. Most schools will generally try to be understanding and accommodate adaptations to the uniform.

If you have a special uniform requirement you should discuss it with your teacher or head teacher. Explain why you want to wear the special item. Don't get angry or upset if they say it is against the school's uniform code. Ask to discuss the code and see if there is a way you can compromise, and meanwhile stick to the school dress code.

# Street-wear aware

Out of school you have a legal right to wear the clothing of your choice without being shouted at, insulted or harassed. If people stare, ignore them. Don't engage them in conversation. If they start to insult you or physically threaten you, find a safe place, such as a library, Post Office, shop or police station. Wait until the threat has gone. If you are threatened by people from your school, report it to the school. If you are threatened by members of your local community, tell your family and report it to the police.

## TALKBACK!

How do you feel about people wearing clothing that reflects their culture and beliefs?

*If people want to fit in with our society they should wear what we wear.*

*Everyone should be able to wear the clothes that they feel comfortable in or that make a statement about them and their beliefs.*

# Prejudice and discrimination

Prejudice, discrimination and racism are negative feelings that are held against another country, culture, people or race.

## Prejudice

When someone is prejudiced, they have a negative opinion about a person or country that is not based on fact or their own experience. It could be an opinion they learnt from their friends or family, read about online or heard on television. People can be prejudiced against many things, such as race, religion, age, gender and sexual orientation.

## Discrimination

Surveys have shown that job applications from people with Asian, Polish or Muslim sounding names are often ignored. This is just one sort of discrimination and is unfair and unjust. If you see prejudice or discrimination happening at school with friends at home or in the community, talk to an adult about it.

# Racism

Racism is when someone is bullied or discriminated against because of their race. Racist insults can be about the colour of people's skin, the clothes they wear or the food they eat. Racism often develops because people don't understand a different culture or they are frightened that another culture is going to take over or isn't like theirs. This could mean that the indigenous community are scared that black and minority ethnic (BME) and newer immigrants might take their jobs or houses, but there is no proof to back up these fears. Some groups deliberately set out to stir up hatred. For example, ISIS fighters release videos that encourage hatred towards non-Muslim communities in order to further their own causes, while far right groups stir up hatred among white people against ethnic communities.

> *If they don't like you for being yourself, be yourself even more.*
>
> Taylor Swift (b. 1989), singer

### Report bullying

Racism and racist bullying is against the law and should never be tolerated, whether it's online, at home, in school or on the streets. Racist bullying should always be reported to the police or a trusted adult.

# DEALING WITH PREJUDICE

To some extent we're all influenced by the attitudes and prejudices of the people around us, our family and friends, teachers and religious leaders.

## Divided community

If we live in an area that has divided communities, it is very easy to become negative and suspicious about each other. We may live side by side every day, but what do we really know about each other? We see reports in the media about people who behave and dress differently from us, have a different religion and speak a different language, and that can make us feel nervous or superior. People from a strict migrant culture watching reports of young white teenagers getting drunk in the street may be disgusted and think that all young white people behave in this way. A newspaper report might say that immigrants are only here to receive benefits and free housing. Do these reports truly represent that community?

## Question everything

We should all question what we read and see online and in the media. Often stories have been exaggerated to increase the drama, or someone ...ne has a reason to create hatred and division. It is difficult to question ...y prejudices, but ask your family why they have their opinions about ...ther culture – are they based on fact or what a newspaper says? ...and engage with people from other communities if you can. ...sit their shops and markets, or see if a local religious or ...mmunity centre has an open day. People and communities ...hrive when they can work and live together peacefully.

# Ban bullying

Most schools have pupils from many different cultures. This is a great way to learn about other cultures first-hand and to introduce those who are new to your school to your own culture. You might be surprised at how similar you are. If you have friends who are prejudiced, talk to them. Find out what their opinions are based on. If people are being nasty or rude to an individual, don't join in. Ask them how they would feel if someone treated them in this way. If the situation gets nasty or violent, call an adult. Don't make racist jokes or comments online or 'like' those who do.

**Smile** and say **hello** if you have a new migrant neighbour – they are probably feeling *isolated* among strangers.

TALKBACK!

How do you think the media can report responsibly on immigration and migrants?

They need to report the facts as they are and not include any personal views. Facts can't be wrong.

Facts can be manipulated. One newspaper can make the facts seem positive and another report can make the same facts seem negative.

# RESPECT!

Living in a multicultural society can open new worlds to all of us and expand our horizons if we work together to develop respect and understanding.

## Open mind

Some people think that their way of living, their religion and their culture is the best. It may be for them, but everyone has the right to live in the way they choose as long as it is within the law. People can be afraid of new things, or refuse to understand new ideas for lots of reasons. Living in a multicultural society can be a challenge for both the indigenous population and the BME and newer immigrants. We all need to keep an open mind about new cultures and be prepared to discuss our beliefs and values with each other. We don't have to agree with each other all the time, but we should respect our differences.

# Pride

It can be very lonely and confusing when you move to a new country. Your instinct is to stay close to your own community. School is an opportunity to make new friends and learn about your new country and culture. But you should not be embarrassed or afraid to talk about where you have come from and your old culture.

> Be **proud** of who you are and where you are from but be prepared to *learn* new things as well.

TALKBACK!

How would you overcome the issues given here?

People stare at me and give me funny looks so I am embarrassed and unsure about approaching them. I stick with my own people because they understand me.

I would like to find out more about the new migrants who live next door, but they ignore me. I don't think they want to get to know us.

## Understanding

True tolerance comes from understanding different cultures. Understanding a culture is not just about what we see on the news or read online. It is about observing for ourselves how different people live and talking to them. Likewise, immigrants coming into another country should learn about and understand that country's culture, beliefs and history.

# SO, TO RECAP...

This is a recap of the issues we have discussed in this book. They are presented as ideas to discuss. Talking things through can help us to understand how we react to situations and feel about them, and help us to get an idea of how other people feel.

## You are your culture

Culture is the way we live, our behaviour, values and beliefs. It covers everything from the food we eat to the art we create and the types of houses we build. Your culture is part of who you are. How do you think people feel who have to leave their country and culture behind and live in a new one that might be very different from their own? Do you think this might make them feel sad, scared and alone? How do you think you would feel if you had to leave your country for good?

## Changes

The new people moving into the country bring their own values and beliefs with them and this can change the indigenous culture. Why does this happen? Do you think it is a good or a bad thing or a bit of both?

## The right to be different

Stereotyping is assuming that all people who look or dress a certain way behave the same. This is a lazy way of thinking that is based on prejudice. Do you think that online reports and videos and the media encourage stereotyping? Do you think they do it deliberately?

## Fight prejudice

We live in a multicultural society, which means that we need to be tolerant and understanding. We should oppose prejudice, discrimination and racism. What are the best ways to tackle these? Why is it so hard to fight negative opinions about different cultures?

## Generation gap?

People who move to a new country may have a really tough time getting used to the new culture and way of life. Why do you think their children and grandchildren will find it much easier? Do you think it's possible for generations who follow two different cultures to live peacefully in the same house and family?

## Clothes are us!

Our clothes are a statement of who we are and what we stand for. Uniforms tell people which school we go to and sport kits show which club we belong to. Some cultures have very specific items of clothing, such as a hijab, turban or patka, that reflect their beliefs. Do you think it's wrong to stop people wearing these clothes? Might some people feel uncomfortable with others wearing clothes very different from their own?

## One culture?

Some people think that new cultures might take over. How do you think different cultures can thrive together in the same society? Do you think that eventually all the different cultures might merge to become one national culture?

# Glossary

**biological characteristic** a physical feature, such as hair or eye colour, inherited from the family

**BME** an abbreviation for black and minority ethnic

**democratic society** where the government is chosen by the people in free elections. The society supports equal rights, freedom of speech, fair trials under the law and tolerates the views of minorities

**discrimination** unfair treatment of someone based on their colour, religion, sex, age, etc.

**ethnic minority** a group that has a different culture from the majority of the indigenous population

**female circumcision** when part or all of the outside of the female genitals are cut away

**first-generation migrants** the children of people who migrated to a country

**forced marriage** when a young person, usually a girl, is forced to marry against her wishes

**hate crimes** crimes committed against a person because of their race, religion, gender or other prejudice

**homophobia** hatred, fear or prejudice against gay, lesbian or bisexual people

**human rights** rights, such as the right of freedom and to live in safety, that belong to every person regardless or their race, gender or religion

**humanitarian issues** problems or situations that affect the wellbeing of humans

**migration** leaving your own country and going to live in another country permanently

**immoral** not behaving in a way that is regarded as correct or acceptable

**indigenous** the population that originally belongs to a place

**integrate** to combine or become part of

**ISIS** also known as Islamic State, an extremist militant Islamic group

**Judaism** the religion of Jewish people

**manipulate** to control, persuade or influence someone in an unfair way

**migrate** to move from one place or country to another

**mixed marriage** a marriage between people of two different races or religions

**morals** right or wrong behaviour

**multiculturalism** a society made up of many different cultures

**oppression** the prolonged cruel or unjust treatment of a group or person

**prejudice** an unfair or unjust opinion that is not based on knowledge or experience

**racism** treating people badly because they are from a different race

**rituals** a way of doing things in a certain order

**stereotype** to fit someone into a specific group of people based on their looks, behaviour etc., rather than actual knowledge of the individual

**traditions** beliefs and ways of doing things passed down from one generation to another

**values** a way of judging what is important to you and how you live

*Learning new words helps you to express your opinions and to understand what you read in this book.*

# Further information

Note to parents and teachers: every effort has been made by the Publishers to ensure websites are suitable for children, that they are of the highest educational value, and that they contain no inappropriate or offensive material. However, because of the nature of the Internet, it is impossible to guarantee that the contents of these sites will not be altered. We strongly advise that Internet access is supervised by a responsible adult.

## WEBSITES AND HELPLINES

If you feel overwhelmed by any of the issues you've read about in this book or need advice check out a website or call a helpline and talk to someone who will understand.

### https://karmanirvana.org.uk/about/

A charity helping young people who are threatened with forced marriage and other honour-based abuse. They can arrange school visits to raise awareness of these issues.

### www.nhs.uk/conditions/female-genital-mutilation-fgm/

An NHS site explaining FGM and why it is dangerous. You can download a statement opposing FGM that makes it very clear that anyone involved in FGM is breaking the law.

### www.gov.uk/stop-forced-marriage

A government website to help those who are in a forced marriage or who are being threatened with a forced marriage. There is a special email address: fmu@fco.gov.uk and telephone: 020 7008 0151; from overseas: +44 (0)20 7008 0151. Advice is given in several different languages.

### www.nspcc.org.uk/preventing-abuse/child-abuse-and-neglect/female-genital-mutilation-fgm/

A 24/7 helpline for anyone fearing FGM. Read more about FGM and hear stories from girls who have survived it. See phone line below or email: fgmhelp@nspcc.org.uk

### www.supportline.org.uk

A charity giving emotional support to children and young people.

### www.familylives.org.uk/advice/primary/health-and-development/culture/

Advice on how to cope with family situations arising from cultural differences at home.

### www.globalkidsoz.com.au

Books and online articles promoting cultural integration.

### www.racismnoway.com.au

Lesson ideas, puzzles, games and loads more about racism and cultural diversity.

### Karma Nirvana
Telephone: 0800 5999247
Phone in confidence if you are being forced into a marriage or suffering from honour-based abuse.

### NSPCC
Telephone: 0800 028 3550
Special FGM helpline, free, anonymous, 24/7.

### www.childline.org.uk
Telephone: 0800 1111

### www.samaritans.org
Telephone: 08457 90 90 90

## READ MORE

www.teachers.org.uk/files/Muslim_Uniforms_4394_0.pdf
The National Union of Teachers guidelines that help to explain the school policy on wearing the hijab and other Islamic dress in school.

*Kids Like Me: Voices of the Immigrant Experience*
by Judith Bloom, Intercultural Press, 2006
The stories of young people who have migrated for many reasons and from many different countries.

*Dealing with Differences*
Susan Martineau, Franklin Watts, 2011
An introduction to how people are different.

29

# Index